Instant Cartoons
for Church Newsletters

5

George W. Knight *Compiler*

BAKER BOOK HOUSE

Grand Rapids, Michigan 49516

A New Book of Instant Chuckles

When *Instant Cartoons for Church Newsletters* was published by Baker Book House several years ago, I had no idea that this would lead to four more books. This fifth compilation of all new and fresh material is designed to generate healthy laughter about church life among readers of local church publications. I'm delighted these tasteful cartoons are meeting a need among churches of many different denominations.

This book introduces the work of a new cartoonist to the series—Charles Dampeer. Charles admits he has been inspired in his cartooning by his friend and fellow minister, Joe McKeever. Joe's work has appeared in all five of the books in this series. Also featured in this book is the work of Howard Paris, who has been making people laugh with his humorous drawings for more than forty years. I think you will agree that these three have a knack for highlighting the humorous side of church life.

My thanks to you for making this series of cartoon books a success. We hope you find this compilation just as funny and useful as the others in the series.

George W. Knight

About the Cartoonists . . .

Charles Dampeer, pastor of the First Baptist Church in Herrin, Illinois, has also served churches in Mississippi and Georgia. He lives by the philosophy that "we need to see humor rather than trouble in many church situations."

Howard Paris is the creator of two books of *Clip-Art Panel Cartoons 1* and *Clip-Art Panel Cartoons 2* published by Baker Book House. With George Knight he has produced the popular *Clip-Art Features for Church Newsletters,* also published by Baker. A former staff artist for the *Atlanta Constitution,* he does free-lance cartooning from his home studio in Mableton, Georgia, a suburb of Atlanta.

Joe McKeever is pastor of the First Baptist Church in Charlotte, North Carolina. He drew the cartoons for another Baker book, *Clip-Art Announcement Panels.* He creates cartoons that appear regularly in Southern Baptist newspapers as well as several general religious publications.

"THE SERMON TODAY IS ON CHOCOLATE PIE — THERE'S NO TEXT FOR IT, BUT WHEN A THING'S RIGHT YOU KNOW IT!"

"TELL ME WHY A KID WHO WADES IN EVERY PUDDLE HE SEES — AND LOVES TO SWIM — PANICS WHEN HE'S BAPTIZED!"

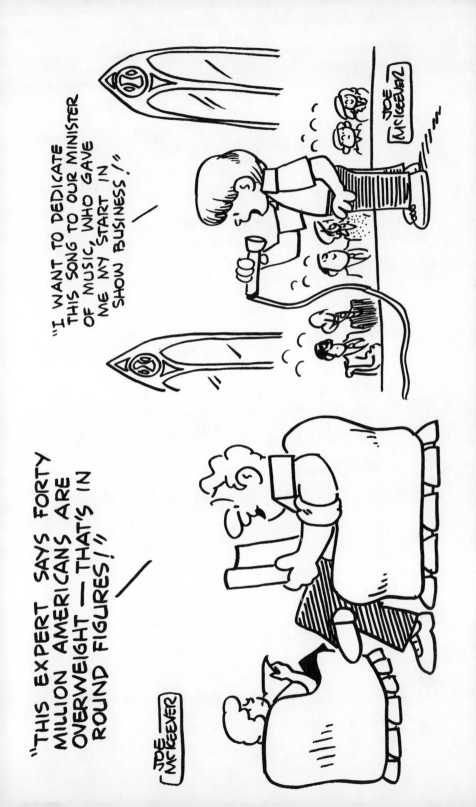

"THE NEWS TONIGHT MAY BE TRAUMATIC— SOME OF YOU MAY WANT TO ASK YOUR PASTOR TO STAND BY!"

"WHEN YOU PREACH HERE, SON, YOU HAVE TO SHOUT— THE AGNOSTICS ARE TERRIBLE IN THIS BUILDING!"

PASTOR RAY DESPERATELY TRIES TO
REMEMBER HIS POINTS IN
YESTERDAY'S SERMON: "FEAR NOT."

"HER MINISTRY IS SPEAKING TO WOMEN
ON THE EVILS OF WORKING OUTSIDE
THE HOME. LAST YEAR SHE SPENT 49
WEEKS ON THE ROAD AND MADE
$50,000."

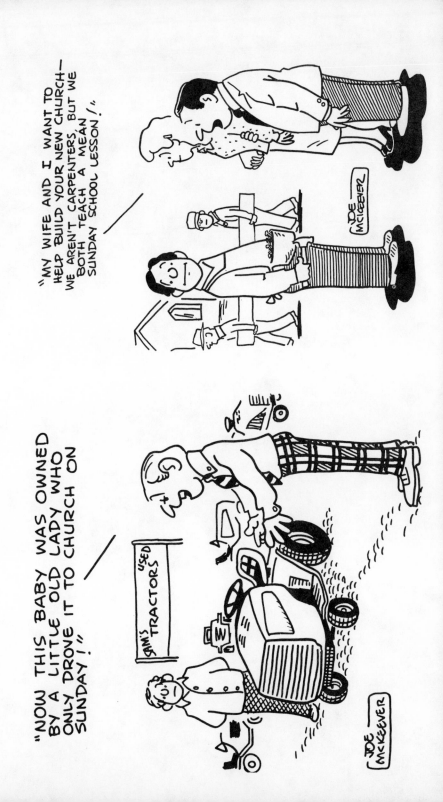

PASTOR RAY COOLS DOWN AFTER A HOT AND POWERFUL SERMON ON HELLFIRE AND BRIMSTONE.

"I'LL NEVER FORGET WHAT MAMA SAID ON HER DEATHBED . . . AH . . . AH . . . HONEY, WHAT WAS IT MAMA SAID?"

"THE PASTOR CALLED—
HIS CALL WAS PUNCTUAL.
HIS WORDS WERE POSITIVE.
HIS CONCERN IS FOR PEOPLE.
HIS NEED IS POWER.
AND YOU'RE BEHIND
IN YOUR PLEDGE!"

JOE MCKEEVER

"IF WE ORDAIN
WOMEN, NEXT THING
YOU KNOW WE'LL
INTERMARRY WITH THEM!"

JOE MCKEEVER

PASTOR RAY COOLS DOWN AFTER A HOT AND POWERFUL SERMON ON HELLFIRE AND BRIMSTONE.

"I'LL NEVER FORGET WHAT MAMA SAID ON HER DEATHBED . . . AH . . . AH . . . HONEY, WHAT WAS IT MAMA SAID?"

"I LIKE BEING WITHOUT A MINISTER. THIS WAY WE CAN DREAM WE MIGHT GET THE PERFECT ONE."

"OUR CHURCH IS COMING TOGETHER. WE'RE ONLY DIVIDED THREE WAYS NOW."

THE CHOIR PREPARES FOR REV. BIG SPLASH'S BAPTISMAL SERVICE.

"YEAH, MAYBE SERVING POPCORN AND SODA IS A RADICAL IDEA, BUT IT SURE HAS INCREASED ATTENDANCE."

"THE CROWD LOOKS A LITTLE SMALL THIS MORNING. HOW ABOUT COUNTING LEGS INSTEAD OF BODIES?"

"SO, I WANT THE CHURCH TO KNOW EXACTLY WHERE I STAND ON THE ISSUE. SOMETIMES I THINK YES, SOMETIMES I THINK NO, AND SOMETIMES I DON'T KNOW."

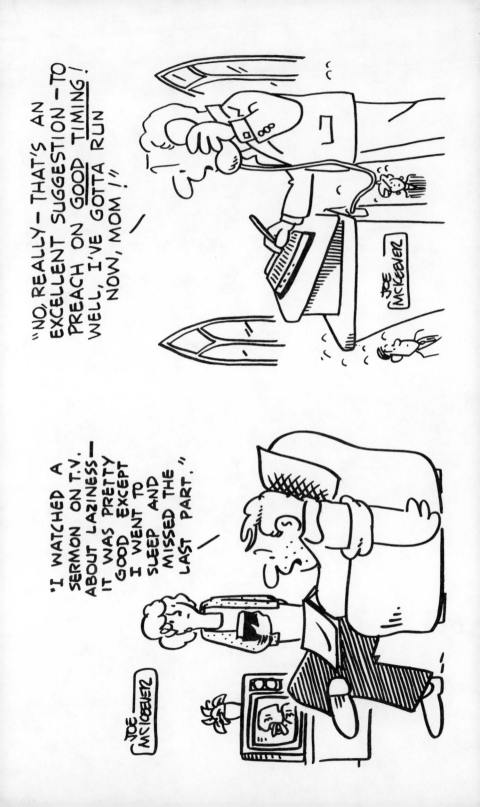

"THE CROWD LOOKS A LITTLE SMALL THIS MORNING. HOW ABOUT COUNTING LEGS INSTEAD OF BODIES?"

"SO, I WANT THE CHURCH TO KNOW EXACTLY WHERE I STAND ON THE ISSUE. SOMETIMES I THINK YES, SOMETIMES I THINK NO, AND SOMETIMES I DON'T KNOW."

"ISN'T OUR PASTOR WONDERFUL? HE JUST KEEPS PREACHING UNTIL HE FINDS A POINT."

"MAYBE IF THE FOREIGN MISSION GIFTS GO UP, WE'LL GET A JEEP FOR TRANSPORTATION NEXT YEAR."

"WE'RE REALLY GETTING INTO BIBLE STUDY. LAST WEEK WE STUDIED 'WERE THE EPISTLES THE WIVES OF THE APOSTLES?'"

"I'LL LAY YOU ODDS HE'S AGAINST GAMBLING."

"IN LAST SUNDAY'S SERMON THE PASTOR SAID TO SMELL THE ROSES ALONG THE WAY. I SEE THE FLOWER COMMITTEE PICKED RIGHT UP ON IT."

"THE WEDNESDAY NIGHT FELLOWSHIP MEAL SURE HAS CHANGED SINCE THE ANIMAL ACTIVIST COUPLE JOINED THE CHURCH."

"OUR MOST SUCCESSFUL MINISTRY IS THE MINISTRY OF REACTION."

"NEVER TRUST A MAN WHO SMILES WHILE PREACHING A SERMON ON HELL."

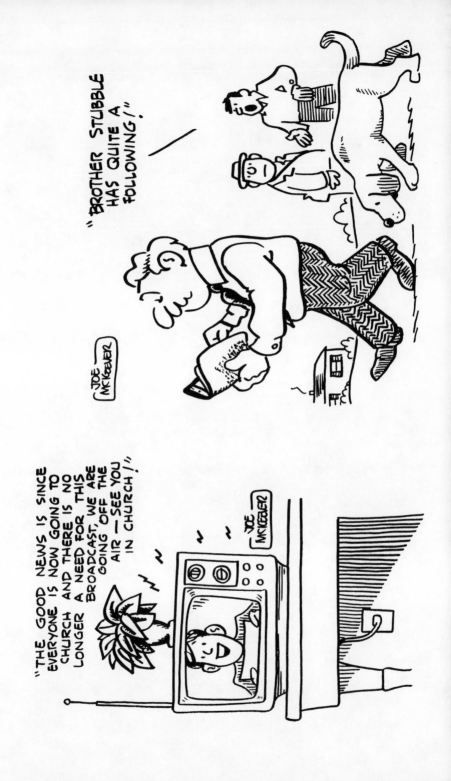

"WILL THERE BE SOUND SYSTEMS IN HEAVEN?"

"MY CHURCH LOVES ME. SHE LOVES ME NOT."

"HER MINISTRY IS SPEAKING TO WOMEN ON THE EVILS OF WORKING OUTSIDE THE HOME. LAST YEAR SHE SPENT 49 WEEKS ON THE ROAD AND MADE $50,000."

PASTOR RAY DESPERATELY TRIES TO REMEMBER HIS POINTS IN YESTERDAY'S SERMON: "FEAR NOT."

"OUR CHURCH IS COMING TOGETHER. WE'RE ONLY DIVIDED THREE WAYS NOW."

"I LIKE BEING WITHOUT A MINISTER. THIS WAY WE CAN DREAM WE MIGHT GET THE PERFECT ONE."

"MY SERMON WILL BE ON THE EFFECT OF INFLATION ON THE CHURCH — AND IT WILL HAVE EIGHTY-THREE POINTS!"

"YOU WANT ME TO SAY SOMETHING GOOD ABOUT THAT SERMON? — WELL, IT DOESN'T CAUSE CANCER, ACID RAIN, OR HARM TO THE OZONE LAYER."

"WE'RE HERE TO REFEREE THE BUSINESS MEETING TONIGHT."

"SO I SAID TO THE PASTOR, 'JUST BECAUSE NO ONE LIKES YOU IS NO REASON TO BE PARANOID.'"

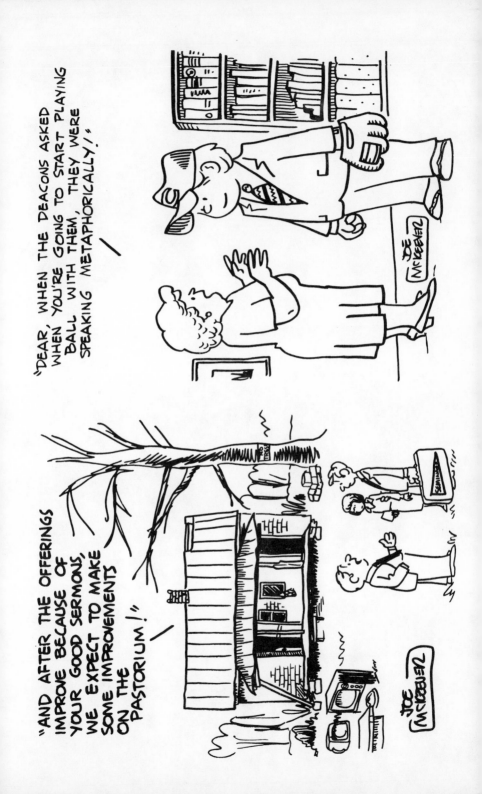

"SO I SAID TO THE PASTOR, 'JUST BECAUSE NO ONE LIKES YOU IS NO REASON TO BE PARANOID.'"

"WE'RE HERE TO REFEREE THE BUSINESS MEETING TONIGHT."

"YEAH, MAYBE SERVING POPCORN AND SODA IS A RADICAL IDEA, BUT IT SURE HAS INCREASED ATTENDANCE."

THE CHOIR PREPARES FOR REV. BIG SPLASH'S BAPTISMAL SERVICE.

"AND AFTER THE OFFERINGS IMPROVE BECAUSE OF YOUR GOOD SERMONS, WE EXPECT TO MAKE SOME IMPROVEMENTS ON THE PASTORIUM!"

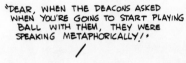

"DEAR, WHEN THE DEACONS ASKED WHEN YOU'RE GOING TO START PLAYING BALL WITH THEM, THEY WERE SPEAKING METAPHORICALLY!"

"WE HAVE THE MOST POPULAR CEMETERY IN THE COUNTY — IN FACT, WHENEVER PEOPLE MENTION OUR CHURCH, THEY AUTOMATICALLY THINK OF DEATH!"

"WHY DON'T ALL OF YOU COME OVER TO CHILDREN'S CHURCH? WE ENJOY OURSELVES OVER THERE!"

"ISN'T OUR PASTOR WONDERFUL? HE JUST KEEPS PREACHING UNTIL HE FINDS A POINT."

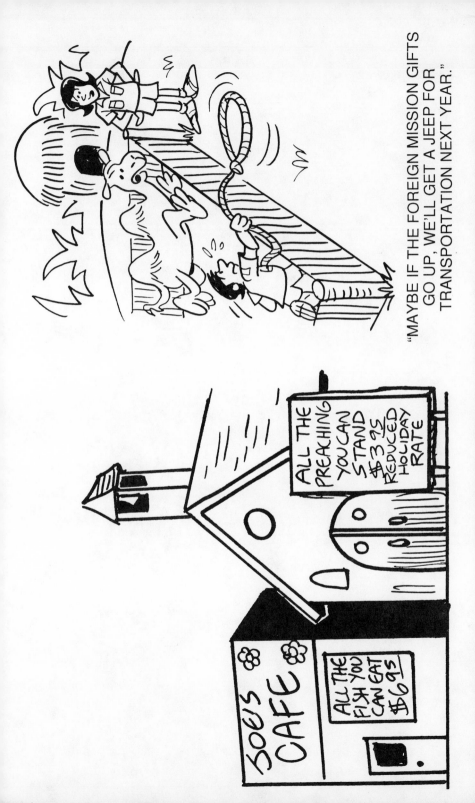

"MAYBE IF THE FOREIGN MISSION GIFTS GO UP, WE'LL GET A JEEP FOR TRANSPORTATION NEXT YEAR."

"THE PASTOR SEEMS TO HAVE A LITTLE ATTITUDE PROBLEM."

"SOMETIMES I THINK OUR PASTOR IS TOO DIRECT."

"SEE, WE DON'T NEED A NEW BUILDING. A LITTLE INNOVATION GOES A LONG WAY."

"THE PASTOR SEEMS TO HAVE A LITTLE ATTITUDE PROBLEM."

"SOMETIMES I THINK OUR PASTOR IS TOO DIRECT."

"I'LL LAY YOU ODDS HE'S AGAINST GAMBLING."

"WE'RE REALLY GETTING INTO BIBLE STUDY. LAST WEEK WE STUDIED 'WERE THE EPISTLES THE WIVES OF THE APOSTLES?'"

"SEE, WE DON'T NEED A NEW BUILDING. A LITTLE INNOVATION GOES A LONG WAY."

"IN LAST SUNDAY'S SERMON THE PASTOR SAID TO SMELL THE ROSES ALONG THE WAY. I SEE THE FLOWER COMMITTEE PICKED RIGHT UP ON IT."

"THE WEDNESDAY NIGHT FELLOWSHIP MEAL SURE HAS CHANGED SINCE THE ANIMAL ACTIVIST COUPLE JOINED THE CHURCH."

"WE REGRET TO ANNOUNCE THAT OUR FAITHFUL MEMBER, MR. BOGGLE, BROKE HIS LEG WHEN HE TRIPPED OVER HIS PERFECT ATTENDANCE SUNDAY SCHOOL PINS."

"I GET THE FEELING YOU DON'T SPEND A LOT OF TIME IN YOUR STUDY."

"OUR MOST SUCCESSFUL MINISTRY IS
THE MINISTRY OF REACTION."

"NEVER TRUST A MAN WHO SMILES
WHILE PREACHING A SERMON ON
HELL."

"WE REGRET TO ANNOUNCE THAT OUR
FAITHFUL MEMBER, MR. BOGGLE,
BROKE HIS LEG WHEN HE TRIPPED
OVER HIS PERFECT ATTENDANCE
SUNDAY SCHOOL PINS."

"I GET THE FEELING YOU DON'T SPEND
A LOT OF TIME IN YOUR STUDY."

"HE HAS AN UNUSUAL TALENT. HE CAN RUN AN IDEA THROUGH HIS MOUTH BEFORE TAKING IT THROUGH HIS MIND."

"LOOKS LIKE THE PASTOR IS GETTING SERIOUS ABOUT THE ATTENDANCE DRIVE."

"HI, MOM—I SAW OUR MINISTER DOWN THE STREET AND INVITED HIM TO DINNER TONIGHT."

"HE HAS AN UNUSUAL TALENT. HE CAN RUN AN IDEA THROUGH HIS MOUTH BEFORE TAKING IT THROUGH HIS MIND.'

"LOOKS LIKE THE PASTOR IS GETTING SERIOUS ABOUT THE ATTENDANCE DRIVE."

"HI, MOM—I SAW OUR MINISTER DOWN THE STREET AND INVITED HIM TO DINNER TONIGHT."

"DON'T YOU JUST **LOVE** SPRING WHEN GOD'S GREAT EARTH BEGINS TO BURST FORTH IN NEW LIFE?"

"HE'S A GREAT MOTIVATOR!"

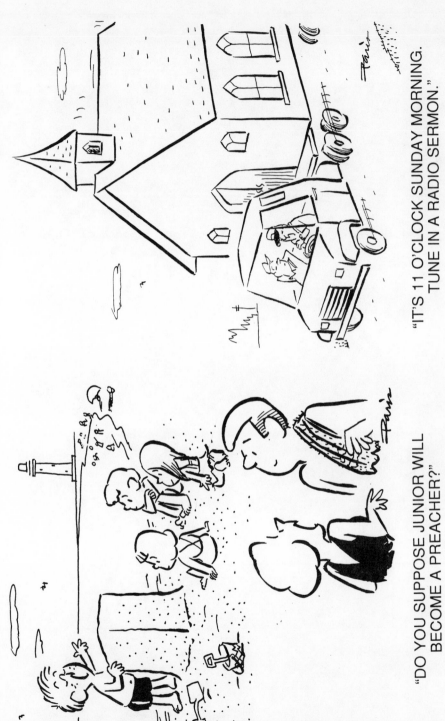

"IT'S 11 O'CLOCK SUNDAY MORNING. TUNE IN A RADIO SERMON."

"DO YOU SUPPOSE JUNIOR WILL BECOME A PREACHER?"

"HE'S A GREAT MOTIVATOR!"

"DON'T YOU JUST **LOVE** SPRING WHEN GOD'S GREAT EARTH BEGINS TO BURST FORTH IN NEW LIFE?"

"DO YOU SUPPOSE JUNIOR WILL BECOME A PREACHER?"

"IT'S 11 O'CLOCK SUNDAY MORNING. TUNE IN A RADIO SERMON."

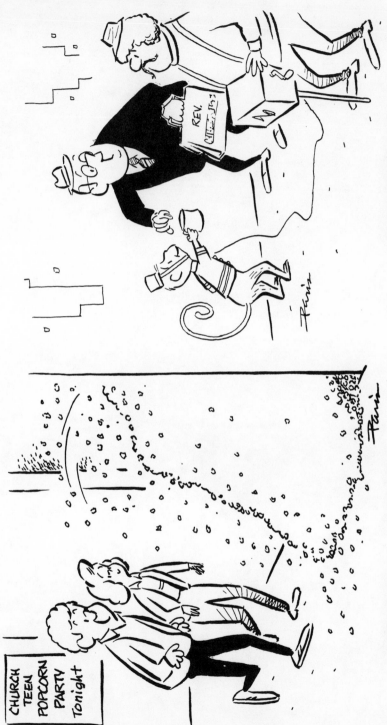

"DOES HE TITHE?"

"THIS MUST BE THE ROOM."

"DOES HE TITHE?"

"THIS MUST BE THE ROOM."

"WELL, IF THEY **HADN'T** ATTACKED, HEAVEN ONLY KNOWS WHEN THE THANKSGIVING SERMON WOULD HAVE ENDED."

"I HOPE THE CHURCH HAS BEEN PUTTING SOMETHING ASIDE FOR A RAINY DAY."

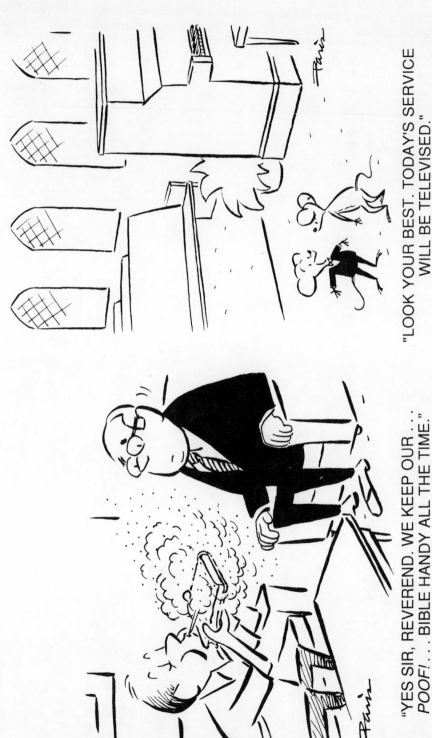

"YES SIR, REVEREND. WE KEEP OUR . . . . POOF! . . . BIBLE HANDY ALL THE TIME."

"LOOK YOUR BEST. TODAY'S SERVICE WILL BE TELEVISED."

"THE WALLS OF JERICHO FELL DOWN FROM LESS THAN THIS!"

"FRANKLY, THIS MAKES ME A LITTLE NERVOUS."

"YES SIR, REVEREND. WE KEEP OUR . . .
POOF! . . . BIBLE HANDY ALL THE TIME."

"LOOK YOUR BEST. TODAY'S SERVICE
WILL BE TELEVISED."

"FRANKLY, THIS MAKES ME A LITTLE
NERVOUS."

"THE WALLS OF JERICHO FELL DOWN
FROM LESS THAN THIS!"

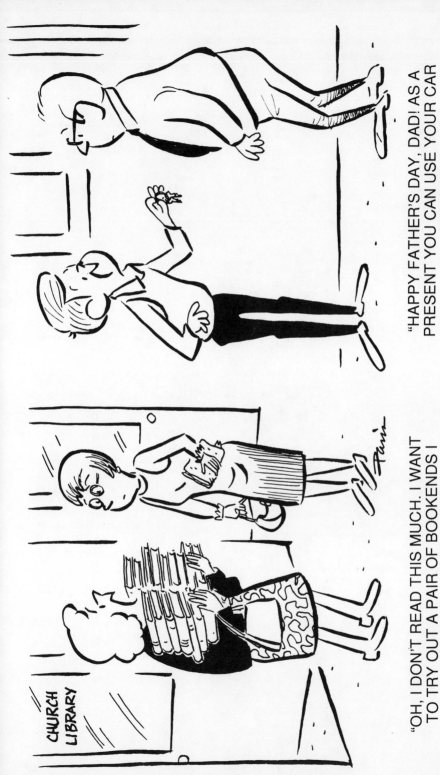

"OH, I DON'T READ THIS MUCH. I WANT TO TRY OUT A PAIR OF BOOKENDS I GOT FOR CHRISTMAS."

"HAPPY FATHER'S DAY, DAD! AS A PRESENT YOU CAN USE YOUR CAR TODAY."

"I UNDERSTAND THERE ARE SEVERAL PROSPECTS HERE FOR OUR CHILDREN'S BIBLE CLASSES."

"I HOPE YOU LIKE IT. THAT'S WHAT I'D WANT FOR MOTHER'S DAY."

"OH, I DON'T READ THIS MUCH. I WANT TO TRY OUT A PAIR OF BOOKENDS I GOT FOR CHRISTMAS."

"HAPPY FATHER'S DAY, DAD! AS A PRESENT YOU CAN USE YOUR CAR TODAY."

"I HOPE YOU LIKE IT. THAT'S WHAT **I'D** WANT FOR MOTHER'S DAY."

"I UNDERSTAND THERE ARE SEVERAL PROSPECTS HERE FOR OUR CHILDREN'S BIBLE CLASSES."

"I DON'T KNOW WHY THE TEACHER WAS SO UPSET. IT'S ONE OF GOD'S CREATURES."

"I'M CURIOUS. IS THERE SOMEONE HERE WHO SAID IF HE EVER CAME TO CHURCH THE ROOF WOULD CAVE IN?"

"DON'T LET ALL THE COMPLIMENTS CONFUSE YOU. IT JUST MEANS YOU'RE TO FURNISH OUR NEXT BUSINESS MEETING REFRESHMENTS."

"YOU'LL BE FINE, DEAR. EVERYBODY'S A LITTLE NERVOUS THE FIRST TIME THEY HAVE TO GIVE DEVOTIONS."

"I'M CURIOUS. IS THERE SOMEONE HERE WHO SAID IF HE EVER CAME TO CHURCH THE ROOF WOULD CAVE IN?"

"I DON'T KNOW WHY THE TEACHER WAS SO UPSET. IT'S ONE OF GOD'S CREATURES."

"DON'T LET ALL THE COMPLIMENTS CONFUSE YOU. IT JUST MEANS YOU'RE TO FURNISH OUR NEXT BUSINESS MEETING REFRESHMENTS."

"YOU'LL BE FINE, DEAR. EVERYBODY'S A LITTLE NERVOUS THE FIRST TIME THEY HAVE TO GIVE DEVOTIONS."

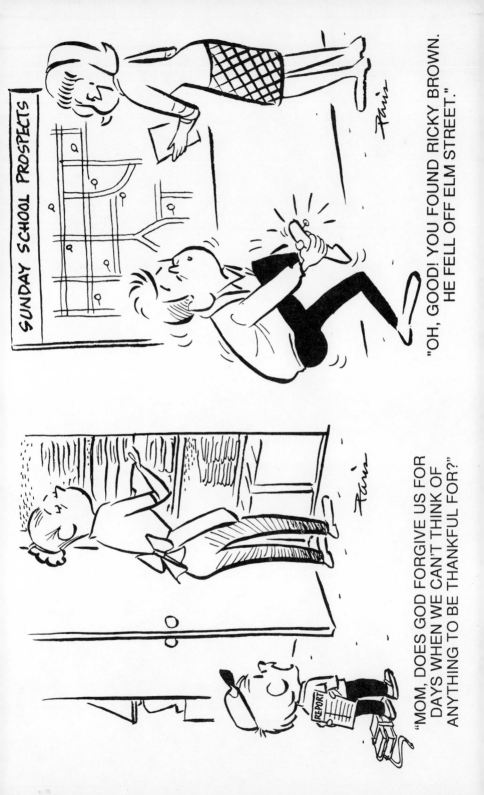

"MOM, DOES GOD FORGIVE US FOR DAYS WHEN WE CAN'T THINK OF ANYTHING TO BE THANKFUL FOR?"

"OH, GOOD! YOU FOUND RICKY BROWN. HE FELL OFF ELM STREET."

"NOW THIS ONE'S LIKE NEW, FOLKS. IT WAS THE FIRST ROW."

"I'M LIKE YOU, PREACHER. I SPEND A LOT OF TIME ON MY KNEES."

"I'D LIKE A SECOND OPINION. NOW LOOK IT UP IN THE **NEW** TESTAMENT."

"THEY HARMONIZE WELL. LET'S GET THEM IN OUR CHURCH CHOIR."

"COMFORTABLE?"

"THEY HARMONIZE WELL. LET'S GET THEM IN OUR CHURCH CHOIR."

"I'D LIKE A SECOND OPINION. NOW LOOK IT UP IN THE **NEW** TESTAMENT."

"COMFORTABLE?"

"I HATE TO TELL YOU THIS, BUT . . ."

"WHAT DID THEY DO WITH THE DOLLAR I GAVE LAST WEEK?"

"WHAT DID THEY DO WITH THE DOLLAR I
GAVE LAST WEEK?"

"I HATE TO TELL YOU THIS, BUT . . ."